OLD BET

and the Start of the American Circus

Robert M. McClung

Illustrated by Laura Kelly

Morrow Junior Books
NEW YORK

FOR GALE
—R. M. McC.

FOR CONNOR BRYN KELLY
—L. K.

The full-color art was prepared on Bristol board with Windsor-Newton watercolors and Prismacolor pencils.
The text type is 15-point Viceroy.

Text copyright © 1993 by Robert M. McClung.   Illustrations copyright © 1993 by Laura Kelly.

Printed in the United States of America.   1   2   3   4   5   6   7   8   9   10

Library of Congress Cataloging-in-Publication Data   McClung, Robert M.   Old Bet and the start of the American circus / Robert McClung; illustrated by Laura Kelly.   p.   cm.   Summary: Describes the performing career of the elephant Old Bet, whose traveling exhibition under the management of Hackaliah Bailey in the early nineteenth century gave rise to the tradition of the American circus.   ISBN 0-688-10642-0 (trade).—ISBN 0-688-10643-9 (lib. bdg.)   1. Old Bet (Elephant)—Juvenile literature.   2. Circus animals—United States—Juvenile literature.   3. Circus—United States—History—19th century—Juvenile literature.   [1. Old Bet (Elephant)   2. Elephants.   3. Circus animals.   4. Circus—History.]   I. Kelly, Laura, ill.   II. Title.   GV1831.E4M38 1993   791.3′2—dc20   92-11020   CIP   AC

The elephant is not only the largest and most sagacious [quadruped] in the world but...is acknowledged to be the greatest natural curiosity ever offered to the public. The one now offered to the view of the curious is a female....She is fifteen years old...upwards of eight feet high, and weighs more than 6000 pounds. Perhaps the present generation may never have an opportunity of seeing an elephant again, as this is the only one in America, and this, perhaps, is the last visit to this place. Admittance, 25¢. Children ½ price.

Essex Register
Salem, Massachusetts
April 20–27, 1816

The great gray beast plodded along the country road, her big ears fanning back and forth. Beside her was a lanky, bearded man. It was the spring of 1808, and Hackaliah Bailey was taking an elephant home to Somers, a little farming village about fifty miles north of New York City.

In a nearby pasture, a cow mooed a greeting, and the elephant rumbled in reply. On a fence post, a rooster crowed a welcome to the coming day, and she raised her trunk in a salute. Then she paused to pull up a clump of daisies and eat them.

"Come on, Old Bet," the man urged her. "Let's get you home and out of sight before folks are up and about."

Old Bet grunted softly and quickened her pace. She had lived among humans for many years and knew their ways.

Hack chuckled to himself. Farmer, cattleman, merchant, and trader, he was a jack-of-all-trades. A shrewd and resourceful man, he also dabbled in showing curiosities to the public from time to time. And Old Bet was a prize curiosity, all right!

He had bought her in New York City just yesterday from a sea captain who had picked her up in London a few weeks before. Old Bet was tame as a kitten and obedient to every command. Hack had big plans for her.

The rising sun was just beginning to peep over the treetops as they reached the outskirts of the sleeping village. Hack heard a clutter of hooves in the distance, then saw the New York stage coming around a bend in the road.

When the lead horses spied Old Bet, they whinnied shrilly and tried to rear up. Then the other horses caught the fright and all four of them started to gallop, almost out of control. The stage swayed from side to side as it thundered past.

Hack grinned as it disappeared in the distance. "You gave those horses a little scare," he said to Old Bet, "but you didn't let the excitement bother you." Old Bet just sighed.

Urging her along, Hack soon had the elephant lumbering down his lane and into the barnyard. Leading her through the wide barn doors, he tied her to a stout beam. He gave her a pail of water and a generous forkful of hay. "That should hold you for the moment," he told her, patting her side.

He heard a surprised cry behind him and turned to see Fred, his twelve-year-old nephew, coming into the barn. Fred's little dog, Dandy, was beside him. "Wow!" the boy exclaimed. "A real elephant!" His freckled face glowed. "Can I feed her this bun?"

Hack nodded, watching as Old Bet daintily picked the bun out of Fred's hand and put it into her mouth.

Whimpering with excitement, the little brown dog sniffed at Old Bet's front leg, his plumed tail wagging vigorously. The elephant blinked her eyes at Dandy, then gently picked him up with her trunk and hoisted him high in the air. After looking him over, she set him down, just as gently. Hack smiled. Old Bet seemed to have taken to Fred and Dandy right off.

"Well, I never!"

Hack looked up and saw his wife, Elizabeth. Hands on her hips, she was shaking her head in disbelief.

"Whatever will you be thinking of next, Hackaliah!" she exclaimed. "This monster will eat us out of house and home!"

"Pshaw!" Hack responded. "Don't you fret. You'll grow to love Old Bet. And she'll make us rich."

After breakfast, Hack and Fred went back to the barn and set to work, draping red and yellow streamers back and forth among the rafters. Hack wanted to show Old Bet in a carnival setting.

Then, as Fred watched, Hack carefully painted a sign on a big smooth slab of wood. When he was finished, he stood back to admire his work. "That should whet folks' curiosity," he told the boy, "'specially after you spread the word around town about Old Bet."

By early afternoon, a crowd had gathered in the barnyard. At one o'clock, Elizabeth began to collect admission fees and people started to stream into the barn.

Inside, they stood around Old Bet, gaping and exclaiming. Fred kept them from getting too close to her while Hack put the elephant through some simple tricks—kneeling, curling her trunk over her head and trumpeting, pulling a cork out of a bottle and drinking the liquid inside.

One little boy, more daring than the others, darted up and held out a piece of bread. Old Bet politely took it and tucked it into her mouth. Soon everyone was pushing forward to give the elephant a tidbit or to pat her broad side. The crowd loved her, just as Hack had figured.

The days went by, and still the people came. Old Bet enjoyed the crowds, Hack noted. She was a real performer. She liked all the food people gave her, too. More than anything else, she loved Elizabeth's ginger cookies. People always hooted with laughter when she nuzzled in Hack's hip pocket to get the cookie he had hidden there.

Sometimes she went too far in her search for goodies, though. One day, she lifted a wallet from a farmer's pocket and was about to stuff it into her mouth when Hack snatched it away from her, just in time.

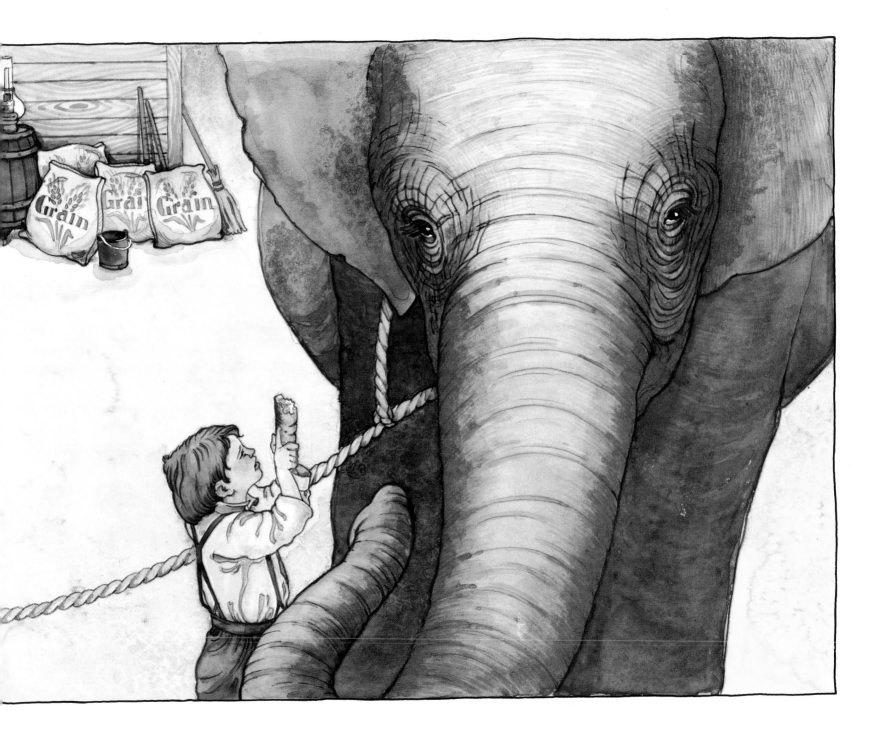

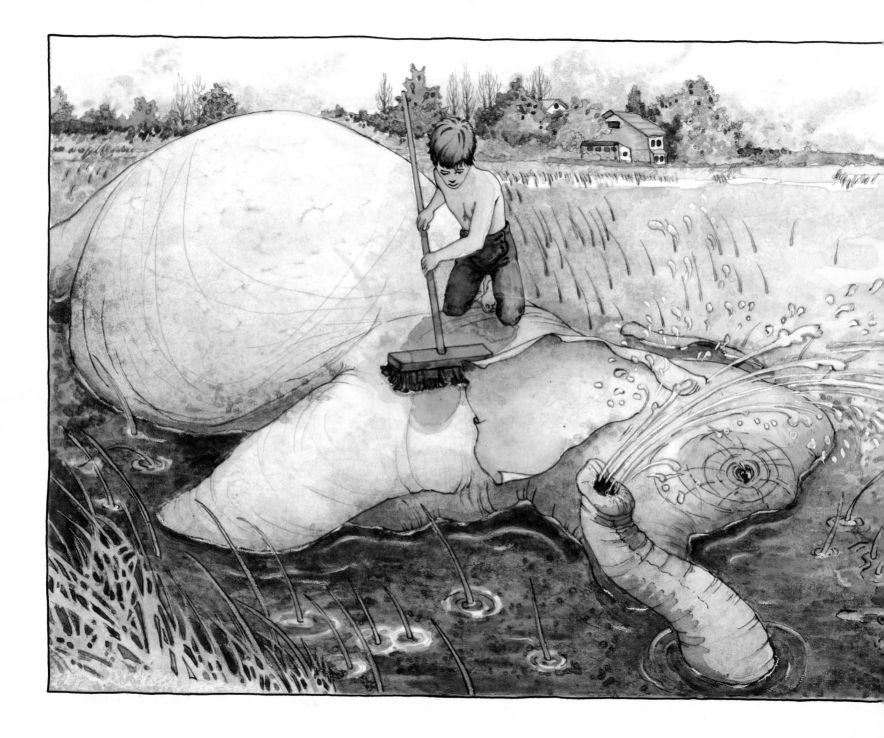

After supper every evening, Fred and Dandy took Old Bet down to the pond in the back pasture. Bullfrogs croaked among the cattails, and ducks quacked indignantly as Old Bet waded in for her daily bath. She would roll over and over in the shallow pond, trumpeting blissfully and spraying water in all directions while Fred scrubbed her sides with a stiff broom. Then the boy would jump in beside Old Bet and join in the fun, swimming circles around her. On the bank, Dandy ran back and forth, wagging his tail and barking with excitement.

By the end of June, the crowds were getting smaller. "'Bout time we took Old Bet on the road," Hack told Fred and Elizabeth at supper one evening. "We'll head out tomorrow night for Jake Quinby's place in Brewster. We'll make it easily by daybreak."

Old Bet performed in Brewster for a week. Then Hack decided they would set out once again, heading for North Salem. Hack drove the wagon loaded with supplies while Fred rode ahead, sitting cross-legged on Old Bet's back. Dandy trotted along beside her. The three of them were inseparable companions now.

The night was dark, and Hack closed his eyes and dozed. Suddenly, a bumping motion roused him, and he realized that they weren't on the road. "Fred, wake up!" he shouted. "Where are we?"

Climbing down from the wagon, Hack hurried forward. Fred was rubbing the sleep out of his eyes, while Old Bet was busy picking up bits of something or other and stuffing them into her mouth.

"Why, she's eating pieces of potatoes," Hack exclaimed. "There's a whole trail of them. Someone's playing a trick on us!"

Up ahead, Hack saw a flicker of flame. The next moment, a big bonfire flared up. As Old Bet walked into the light, Hack saw a huge crowd of people standing near the fire. It looked as if most of the inhabitants of North Salem were there. They were laughing and cheering—and getting a free look at his elephant!

Hack shook his head, then slowly grinned. "You North Salem folks outsmarted us with that potato trail," he admitted. "So take a good look at Old Bet now. Tomorrow's another day."

Old Bet proved a star attraction everywhere she went that summer and fall. When the weather started turning colder, Hack headed for home. By the time winter set in, with lots of snow, Old Bet was snug in the big stall of the stable. Dandy stayed in the barn with Old Bet most of the time, keeping her company.

Everybody kept busy that winter, getting ready for next year's show season. Elizabeth and her quilting group made a beautiful blanket for Old Bet. It was bright red and orange and blue, with a row of golden tassels on either side.

Fred taught Dandy how to dance on his hind legs. Dressed in a red jacket, and with a peaked cap topped with a rooster's long tail feathers tied onto his head, the little dog put on a real show. Then the boy taught Old Bet to lift Dandy onto her back to dance, while she swayed back and forth in time to the music Hack played on his fiddle.

Late that winter, Hack bought two new wagons, which he and Fred painted bright red with yellow trim. Then he had Thaddeus Barlow, the blacksmith, make two strong barred cages and bolt them to the wagon beds. "When spring comes, we'll get some more animals," he told Fred. "We'll have a real menagerie."

True to his word, Hack went to New York City in early April and bought a gentle Russian brown bear named Ivan and an angry old tiger named Nero. Once he was back in Somers, Hack hired two young neighbors to drive the new animal wagons and to help with the show. A few days later, they took to the road for a spring and summer tour through New York State and Connecticut.

As they traveled from town to town, Fred often went ahead to put up posters and pass out handbills. On the day the show was to open at a new location, he dressed up like a clown and marched to the village green, ringing a bell or blowing a horn and turning cartwheels to attract attention. Soon everyone would know that Bailey's traveling show was coming to town.

One morning in June, Hack told Fred to parade Old Bet right down the main street of Danbury, Connecticut. He figured she would be the best advertisement for the show. "Ring your bell, blow your horn," he told the boy. "The young'uns will tag along after you and Old Bet like ducklings after their mother."

And that's exactly what happened! Swarms of excited children and their parents followed Fred and Old Bet right to the doors of the big barn where the rest of the show was housed. That day, Hackaliah Bailey's menagerie performed before a larger crowd than ever before.

One night a week later, as they were heading from New Haven to Wallingford, it began to rain hard. The heavy wagons swayed and lurched through the deep ruts of the dirt road, and their wheels sank into the mud. Old Bet plodded steadily onward. She didn't mind the rain or the mud.

Near midnight, the storm grew worse, with loud claps of thunder and blinding bolts of lightning. Ivan the bear curled up in his cage, silent and miserable, but not Nero the tiger. Excited by the storm, he lashed his tail from side to side and roared.

Then his wagon fell into a deep pothole and almost tipped over. Nero screamed and charged at the bars of the cage, trying to get out. The frightened horses struggled but couldn't pull the wagon out of the deep hole.

"Bring up Old Bet," Hack called out. "She'll get that wagon clear!"

Fred quickly brought the elephant over. Old Bet put her broad forehead against the rear of the wagon and pushed with all her strength while the horses pulled. In no time, the wagon was free!

Except for a few bad moments now and then, the second show season was even more successful than the first. A few other people in the area had started animal shows too, but none of them had Old Bet. She was the star everywhere.

That winter, Hack bought a lion, two trained pigs, and a dancing horse. Now Bailey's Traveling Show and Menagerie was too big to fit into most barns!

Then Hack got an idea. He would put up a high canvas wall around a huge circle of upright posts. "The canvas will enclose the show," he told Fred, "and we won't have to pay rent for barns. Besides, Old Bet can help us put up the posts wherever we go."

Elizabeth and her quilting circle sewed huge pie-shaped pieces of canvas together to make a circular roof for the canvas wall. Held up by a tall center post and tied down with ropes all around, Hack's was the first circus tent.

Every spring, Bailey's Traveling Show and Menagerie set out on a trip through New England and New York State. Hack's show now had more acts, more animals, two clowns, an acrobat, a tightrope walker, and a juggler, as well as a bareback rider for the dancing horse. Fred acted as master of ceremonies and began every performance by leading the parade of performers and animals around the center ring. He rode on Old Bet's back while Dandy sat on his lap.

By 1815, there were a half dozen traveling shows like Hack's in the area, but that was all right with Hack. Plenty of room for them all, he figured. Plus, he had the advantage, for his was the only show with an elephant.

In 1825, Hack took some of the money he had saved and built a handsome red-brick hotel in the center of Somers. He called it the Elephant Hotel in honor of Old Bet, who had made it all possible.

At the crossroads in front of the hotel, he put up a monument to his beloved elephant. Three feet high and four feet long, the gilded carving of Old Bet stood on top of a tall shaft of granite. It was a monument to a good and faithful friend.

When Hack proudly showed the statue to Old Bet, she rumbled deep in her throat, then curved her trunk up to her forehead and trumpeted. After that, she rummaged in Hack's hip pocket and found the ginger cookie he had hidden there for her.

The story of Hackaliah Bailey and Old Bet is based on historical accounts but is told as fiction. Many of the true details lie hidden behind a curtain of conflicting stories and legends. Hackaliah Bailey was a real person, and Old Bet was a real elephant. Records indicate that she probably died before the Elephant Hotel was built.

Today, a visitor to Somers can see the statue of Old Bet and the Elephant Hotel—which now serves as the town hall—right in the center of town. People who live in Somers say that their village is the birthplace of the American circus. Hackaliah Bailey and Old Bet, they declare, were the ones who started it all.